FREEDOM'S PROMISE

W9-DIE-531

THE CHINESE EXCLUSION ACT

AND ITS RELEVANCE TODAY

BY DUCHESS HARRIS, JD, PHD

WITH KATE CONLEY

Core Library

An Imprint of Abdo Publishing
abdobooks.com

Cover image: In the late 1800s, many Americans rioted to protest immigration from China.

abdobooks.com

Published by Abdo Publishing, a division of ABDO, PO Box 398166, Minneapolis, Minnesota 55439. Copyright © 2020 by Abdo Consulting Group, Inc. International copyrights reserved in all countries. No part of this book may be reproduced in any form without written permission from the publisher. Core Library™ is a trademark and logo of Abdo Publishing.

Printed in the United States of America, North Mankato, Minnesota
092019
012020

THIS BOOK CONTAINS
RECYCLED MATERIALS

Cover Photo: MPI/Archive Photos/Getty Images
Interior Photos: MPI/Archive Photos/Getty Images, 1; Apic/Hulton Archive/Getty Images, 5; Everett Historical/Shutterstock Images, 6–7; Red Line Editorial, 9, 39; Hulton Archive/Archive Photos/Stringer, 10; North Wind Picture Archives, 14, 21; Underwood Archives/UIG Universal Images Group/Newscom, 16–17; Buyenlarge/Archive Photos/Getty Images, 18; Smith Collection/Gado/Archive Photos/Getty Images, 26–27, 43; Picture History/Newscom, 29; Fotosearch/Archive Photos/Getty Images, 33; Paul Sakuma/AP Images, 36–37

Editor: Maddie Spalding
Series Designer: Ryan Gale

Library of Congress Control Number: 2019942094

Publisher's Cataloging-in-Publication Data

Names: Harris, Duchess, author. | Conley, Kate, author.
Title: The Chinese exclusion act and its relevance today / by Duchess Harris and Kate Conley
Description: Minneapolis, Minnesota : Abdo Publishing, 2020 | Series: Freedom's promise|
Includes online resources and index.
Identifiers: ISBN 9781532190803 (lib. bdg.) | ISBN 9781532176654 (ebook)
Subjects: LCSH: Chinese Americans--History--Juvenile literature. | Immigrants--United States--History--19th century--Juvenile literature. | Citizenship--Law and legislation--Juvenile literature. | Citizenship--United States--History--Juvenile literature. | Race discrimination--Juvenile literature.
Classification: DDC 305.89510--dc23

CONTENTS

A LETTER FROM DUCHESS

Most people want to feel included. One of the great ideas about the United States of America is that it is a nation that welcomes immigrants. Immigrants can gain citizenship. Citizenship provides legal rights, but it can also provide a sense of belonging. This book tells the story of a time in US history when an entire group of people was excluded.

More than 100 years ago, many Americans discriminated against immigrant groups, including Chinese immigrants. This attitude led to the passage of a law in 1882 called the Chinese Exclusion Act. The Chinese Exclusion Act severely restricted the number of Chinese immigrants allowed into the United States. It also prevented Chinese immigrants from becoming US citizens. For decades, Chinese Americans did not feel welcome in the United States.

Some Americans today still want to stop certain groups of people from coming to the country. As you read this book, I challenge you to think about who has been made to feel excluded in the United States.

In the late 1800s and early 1900s, many Chinese Americans opened shops and businesses.

GOLD MOUNTAIN

In January 1848, gold was discovered in the American River in California. This discovery started what is called the California Gold Rush. Americans flocked to California. They hoped to find gold and become rich. By the summer's end, more than 4,000 people had traveled to California. They set up tents along the banks of the American River. They mined for gold.

Ships that were docked in California's harbors brought news of the discovery to people in other countries. Before long, people from all over the world were traveling to

In the 1800s, Chinese immigrants used special equipment to mine gold.

California to mine for gold. One of the largest groups to arrive came from China.

News of California's gold reached China in 1849. Chinese people traveled to California in ships. They called California *gam saan*. This phrase means "gold mountain." By 1851, approximately 25,000 Chinese immigrants had moved to California to seek their fortunes.

SETTLING IN CALIFORNIA

Before the Gold Rush, few Chinese people lived in the United States. The 1840 US Census listed only four Chinese people in the entire nation. That is because China's borders had been closed for many years. But in 1840, China opened its borders. People could more easily leave China.

News of the Gold Rush arrived in China at a time when life was difficult. China had suffered decades of hardship. People had experienced war, droughts, and floods. And China's population had grown quickly.

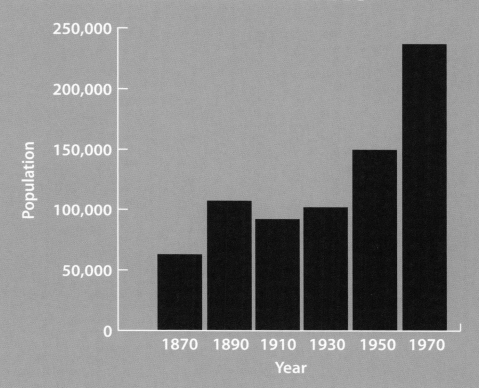

CHINESE AMERICAN POPULATION PATTERNS

The above graph shows the population of Chinese Americans in the United States in certain years. What trends do you notice? How has the Chinese American population changed over time?

This growth drove many people into poverty. They did not have enough food to survive. They wanted to move somewhere where they could have better lives. They were drawn to the promise of gold in California.

Chinese laborers were one of the first groups of immigrants to arrive in California during the Gold Rush.

The voyage from China to California took approximately six weeks. Those who made the trip found a wild and rough land. There were no immigration checkpoints. Immigrants arrived at San Francisco Harbor in California. They did not have to undergo medical exams or file paperwork. As soon as they left the ship, they were on their own. Many of them headed to California's gold fields.

Gold seemed to be on every riverbank. When each area was stripped of easy-to-reach gold, white miners moved on to new land. White people discriminated against Chinese people. They made Chinese people mine the land white miners left behind. The Chinese miners worked hard. They dug deeper to find gold that the white miners had missed.

As more people arrived in California, land became scarce. Gold became harder to find. Camps grew crowded. Miners started to argue over land. White miners blamed Chinese miners for the land loss. They began to resent Chinese immigrants.

THE BURLINGAME TREATY

Anson Burlingame was a US representative and a lawyer. He also served as the US minister to China. He helped create a treaty between China and the United States in 1868. It was called the Burlingame Treaty. It allowed the United States to sell goods in China. In exchange, Chinese immigrants could enter the United States easily. The treaty increased the population of Chinese immigrants in the United States.

They drove Chinese miners from their mines. They stole gold from the Chinese miners.

RAILROAD LABORERS

The difficult conditions in California did not slow Chinese immigration. Nearly 30,000 Chinese immigrants arrived in California between 1860 and 1870. This doubled California's Chinese population. Chinese people faced racism. In order to survive, they had to take jobs that no one else wanted. For many, this meant working on a new government railway project.

In 1862 the US government passed the Pacific Railway Act. It provided funds to build a transcontinental railroad. The Central Pacific Railroad company would begin building in California and move east. The Union Pacific Railroad company would begin building along the Missouri River and move west. The two companies would meet in the middle.

The work to build the railroad was backbreaking. Laborers blasted tunnels through mountains. They built bridges over rivers. They worked in dangerous conditions. Few white Californians wanted the jobs. The Central Pacific Railroad hired thousands of Chinese immigrants.

Despite this contribution, Chinese immigrants soon faced a new problem. They made up a small fraction of the US population. But some Americans accused them of stealing jobs from white people. Under pressure from

Workers used dynamite to blast rocks while building the transcontinental railroad. Many Chinese workers died while building the railroad.

voters, the US government passed a law in 1882. The law was officially called the Immigration Act of 1882. But it was commonly known as the Chinese Exclusion Act. It stopped Chinese laborers from entering the country. Those who remained in the country faced increasing racism and violence.

STRAIGHT TO THE
SOURCE

For many years, the Chinese Exclusion Act was ignored in history books. K. Scott Wong is a historian. He explained why people should study the Chinese Exclusion Act:

> I think it's essential that Americans know about the exclusion of Chinese—not because it's the Chinese, but because it reflects how America has come to develop. And how America saw itself at one time, and how it continues to see itself. It has much to do with the character of our national history. And that, to me, is the most important thing in understanding how we became who we are today. Some of it has to do with the fact that we excluded Chinese for 60 years.

> Source: Ric Burns and Li-Shin Yu. "The Chinese Exclusion Act." *PBS*. PBS, May 29, 2018. Web. Accessed May 2, 2019.

What's the Big Idea?
Take a close look at this passage. Why do you think so few Americans know about the Chinese Exclusion Act? What makes it an important part of American history? How does it reflect American attitudes about immigration?

GROWING MISTRUST

While Chinese immigrants built the transcontinental railroad, the American Civil War (1861–1865) was going on. Many parts of the nation were in ruins after the war ended. Americans began to rebuild. The economy boomed. But this success was short-lived. In 1873 the US economy collapsed.

During this time, many Americans were out of work. It was difficult to find a job. In California, thousands of Chinese immigrants were already out of work. They had lost their jobs after the transcontinental railroad was completed in 1869. Some had opened shops

Chinese Americans opened drug stores and many other types of businesses in the late 1800s.

Chinese immigrants formed a Chinatown neighborhood in Manhattan, New York, in the late 1800s.

or begun to farm. But most joined other Americans in the search for work.

Throughout the country, competition for jobs created mistrust and hatred. Chinese immigrants often accepted less pay than white people. Employers usually hired the cheapest workers. This meant that they sometimes hired immigrants over white Americans.

Chinese immigrants accepted low wages for several reasons. Most did not speak English. This limited their job options. Few had any job skills. And many were in debt. They had borrowed money to pay for their ship fare to the United States. They had to pay back the loan quickly. Family members in China were also counting on them to send money back. The immigrants had no choice but to take whatever work they could find.

TENSIONS AND VIOLENCE

Wage disputes fueled tensions between white and Chinese Americans. These tensions erupted into violence on October 24, 1871. On that night in Los Angeles, California, two Chinese gangs got into a fight. White police officers tried to break it up. But one white man was shot. White residents were outraged. A mob of 500 white people gathered. The Chinese gang members took refuge in a building. But the mob dragged them out of the building. The mob lynched the men. Members of the mob also killed other Chinese residents. They looted and damaged Chinese people's homes. The attack lasted five hours. The mob killed 17 Chinese people. This was 10 percent of the city's Chinese population. Eight men were later charged for their roles in the massacre. But the charges were overturned. This incident ramped up tensions even further.

By the late 1870s, political groups began to call for the forced removal of Chinese immigrants. Denis Kearney led one such group in San Francisco. It was a labor organization called the Workingmen's Party of California. Kearney organized rallies. He roused the crowds by repeating, "The Chinese Must Go!" People who attended these rallies left full of hatred. They burned down Chinese people's properties. They attacked Chinese people on the streets.

In his speeches, Denis Kearney claimed that Chinese immigrants took jobs away from white Americans.

THE CHINESE EXCLUSION ACT

Anti-Chinese feelings in California soon spread to Washington, DC. Californians asked their representatives there to pass a bill. The bill would restrict the immigration of Chinese people to the United States. In 1882 President Chester A. Arthur signed the bill into law. It became the Chinese Exclusion Act.

The Chinese Exclusion Act was the first US law to restrict immigration based on national origin. It stopped all Chinese laborers from entering the United States for ten years. Captains who illegally transported Chinese laborers on their ships could be found guilty of a crime. They had to pay a steep fine for each laborer.

The law also affected Chinese immigrants who already lived in the United States. They needed a special certificate to leave the country and come back. This affected anyone who wanted to go back to China to visit family. The certificate was hard to get. To prevent fraud, agents recorded detailed information about each person. Chinese immigrants who did not have this certificate were not allowed back into the United States.

Before the act was passed, Chinese immigrants could become naturalized. Naturalization is the process of becoming an official citizen of a nation. A citizen has rights that are guaranteed under the law. These include the right to vote and run for elected office. US citizens are also given US passports. The Chinese Exclusion Act kept Chinese immigrants from becoming naturalized. The rights of US citizenship were no longer available to them.

PURGES

Chinese immigrants faced discrimination before the Chinese Exclusion Act. But their situation worsened after the act passed. White people joined together for purges. These were attempts to remove all Chinese people from an area. More than 300 purges happened across the West Coast.

One of the most organized purges happened in Tacoma, Washington, in 1885. On the morning of November 3, hundreds of white men gathered in Tacoma. They walked down the city streets. The crowd stopped at each Chinese-owned home and business. One person knocked on the door. He told the occupants that they were being forced from the city. They were ordered to assemble that afternoon on a street corner.

More than 200 Chinese people gathered there. They were forced to walk many miles to a train station outside of Tacoma. When they arrived, only a small shed served as shelter. Many waited outside in the wind and rain until 3:00 a.m. Then they boarded a train to Portland, Oregon. City leaders had met their goal. There were no more Chinese people in Tacoma. There would not be another Chinese resident in the city until the 1920s.

EXPLORE ONLINE

Chapter Two explores the Chinese immigrant experience in the late 1800s and early 1900s. The article at the website below shows a timeline of Chinese immigration to the United States. How is the information from the website the same as the information in Chapter Two? What new information did you learn from the website?

THE CHINESE EXPERIENCE: TIMELINE
abdocorelibrary.com/chinese-exclusion-act

LIFE UNDER THE ACT

In the late 1800s, many Chinese Americans fought for their rights. Wong Chin Foo was one of the most outspoken Chinese activists at this time. Wong came to the United States in 1867. He became active in politics after the Chinese Exclusion Act passed. He traveled across the United States. He gave speeches. He demanded equal rights for Chinese Americans. He encouraged Chinese Americans to get involved in politics. He fought to repeal, or overturn, the Chinese Exclusion Act.

In 1884 Chinese American Joseph Tape, *left*, sued a school board for not allowing his daughter to enroll in a public school.

Chinese immigrants faced barriers in their fight for equal rights. They could not become citizens. That meant that they could not vote for leaders who might repeal the Chinese Exclusion Act. But they could seek help from the legal system. They challenged the Chinese Exclusion Act. They tried to gain equal rights. Between 1882 and 1905, Chinese Americans filed more than 10,000 court cases against the US government. Of these, about 20 went to the US Supreme Court.

One landmark case was brought to the Supreme Court in 1886. It was called *Yick Wo v. Hopkins*. Yick Wo owned a laundry business. Many Chinese laundries were in wooden buildings. San Francisco passed a law in 1880. It said that people could not operate laundries in wooden buildings unless they had a permit. The city refused to give permits to Chinese laundry owners. But it did give permits to white laundry owners. Yick's laundry was in a wooden building. He continued to run his business without the permit. He was charged with breaking the law.

Many Chinese Americans owned and operated laundries in the late 1800s and early 1900s.

Yick believed he had not broken the law. He pointed to the US Constitution. He used the Fourteenth Amendment to make his argument. This amendment guarantees all people equal protection under the law. The Supreme Court ruled in Yick's favor. It said that laws had to be applied equally to all people.

RENEWING THE ACT

The Chinese Exclusion Act was meant to be temporary. It was supposed to last ten years. But when the law was set to expire, lawmakers decided to renew it. They passed the Geary Act in 1892. This law extended the Chinese Exclusion Act for another ten years. It also created new restrictions. Chinese immigrants had to carry identification cards at all times. Immigrants caught without identification could be deported, or forced to leave the country. Other rules further restricted immigration. Chinese students and teachers were allowed to enter the country. So were diplomats and tourists. All other Chinese immigrants were banned.

In 1902 lawmakers again renewed the Chinese Exclusion Act. They made the act permanent two years later. There was no new expiration date for the ban.

ANGEL ISLAND

Although they faced discrimination, many Chinese people still wanted to move to the United States.

Some wanted to rejoin their families. Others wanted to get an education.

In the early 1900s, Chinese immigrants came to Angel Island. It was an immigration station off the coast of San Francisco. It opened in 1910. Immigrants from more than 80 countries passed through the station. This included immigrants from Australia, Russia, Japan, and Mexico.

Immigrants who arrived at the station were given a medical exam. Then they were assigned a room. The rooms Chinese immigrants were assigned to were

RESISTANCE

The Geary Act required Chinese immigrants to carry photo identification cards. No other group in the United States had to carry such cards. Chinese community leaders discouraged people from registering for the card. This was a form of protest. More than 103,000 Chinese immigrants refused to register. Some Chinese immigrants also challenged the Geary Act. They thought the act violated the US Constitution. They brought their case to the Supreme Court, but they lost.

often overcrowded. Immigrants could not leave the rooms unless they were supervised by a guard. They were kept in these rooms while awaiting an interview.

The interview process was difficult. Immigrants had to answer detailed questions about their family history. Officials wanted to make sure the information on immigrants' documents was correct. They worried that some people would falsify documents to get into the country. Anyone suspected of this crime could be deported.

Deportation was a real fear for many Chinese immigrants. Five percent of Chinese immigrants were deported. For those who were not deported, the immigration process took a long time. Most were processed through Angel Island within two weeks. But some were kept on the island for more than a year.

FURTHER RESTRICTIONS

Angel Island remained open until 1949. Between 1910 and 1949, approximately 100,000 Chinese immigrants

Most of the immigrants who passed through Angel Island were from Asian countries such as China and Japan.

passed through its gates. But within those years, greater restrictions were placed on Chinese immigration. In 1924 the Johnson-Reed Act was passed. This act was commonly known as the Immigration Act of 1924. It banned all Asian immigrants. Then in 1925, the Supreme Court made an exception. Chinese women married to noncitizen Chinese merchants would be allowed into the country. But Chinese wives of US citizens were not allowed entry. This changed in 1930. The US Congress said that Chinese women who had married US citizens before the 1924 act was passed could enter the country. But Chinese immigration was still tightly restricted.

REPEALING THE ACT

Activists helped make the public aware of the ways Chinese people were mistreated. Public opinion slowly began to shift. Then everything changed when World War II (1939–1945) broke out. The United States and China fought on the same side during the war. This changed the relationship between the two nations.

In 1943 the US government repealed the Chinese Exclusion Act. Chinese Americans could become citizens. But immigration was still restricted. A quota limited how many Chinese immigrants could enter the country. It allowed 105 Chinese people into the country each year. This number was small. But it was a sign of progress.

FURTHER EVIDENCE

Chapter Three explores what life was like for Chinese immigrants under the Chinese Exclusion Act. What was one of the main points of the chapter? What evidence is included to support this point? Read the article at the website below. Does the information on the website support this point? Does it present new evidence?

SAN FRANCISCO CHINATOWN
abdocorelibrary.com/chinese-exclusion-act

THE ACT'S LEGACY

The final obstacle to Chinese immigration fell away in 1965. In that year, Congress passed the Immigration and Naturalization Act. It is commonly known as the Hart-Celler Act. It removed immigration quotas based on race. For the first time in decades, Chinese immigrants could arrive in the United States freely.

JUDY CHU

As time passed, the Chinese Exclusion Act began to fade from the public's memory. But not everyone forgot about it. Chinese Americans such as Judy Chu remembered.

Lowe Shee Miu, a Chinese American resident of Oakland, California, stands in front of a monument at Angel Island.

Chu is a representative for California. In 2012 she spoke in front of the US House of Representatives. She asked the House to pass a resolution. The resolution would be an apology. It would express regret for laws that discriminated against Chinese Americans. The House passed the resolution.

RELEVANCE TODAY

Today, Americans are divided on the subject of immigration. Some Americans want to build a wall on the US–Mexico border. Its purpose would be to stop illegal immigration. But many people believe it would unfairly target Mexican immigrants.

CHINESE AMERICAN POPULATIONS IN US CITIES

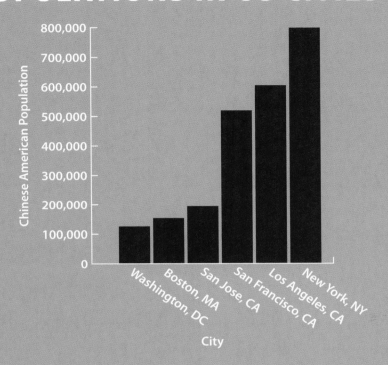

The above graph shows the cities with the largest Chinese American populations as of 2015. In the past, many Chinese immigrants settled along the West Coast. Which parts of the country appear to have the highest Chinese American populations today?

In 2017 President Donald Trump signed orders. The orders tried to ban immigration from Muslim countries to the United States. Many people protested the bans. They believed the bans unfairly targeted Muslims.

ATTITUDES TOWARD IMMIGRANTS

Many immigrant groups have historically been persecuted in the United States. In the mid-1800s, many immigrants from Ireland and Germany came to the United States. A political group called the Know-Nothing party opposed all immigration. During World War II, the United States and Japan were enemies. Americans of Japanese descent were forced to live in prison camps. On September 11, 2001, Muslim terrorists hijacked and crashed airplanes. They killed nearly 3,000 people. Prejudice against Muslims increased after the attacks.

The Chinese Exclusion Act restricted Chinese immigration for many years. But this period is often overlooked. Studying this act could help leaders make better decisions for the future. It could also help Americans understand the role of immigrants in the United States. Immigrants have helped shape the nation. They will continue to do so in the future.

STRAIGHT TO THE
SOURCE

Judy Chu released a statement after the House passed her resolution in 2012. She wrote:

Today the House made history. . . . The Chinese Exclusion Act enshrined injustice into our legal code—it stopped the Chinese . . . from immigrating, from ever becoming naturalized citizens and ever having the right to vote. The last generation of people personally affected by these laws is leaving us, and finally Congress has expressed the sincere regret that Chinese Americans deserve. . . . This is only the fourth time that Congress has passed such a resolution of regret in the last 25 years. This makes today a rare moment in history for the Chinese American Community.

Source: Judy Chu. "House Passes Rep. Judy Chu's Resolution of Regret for the Chinese Exclusion Act." *United States House of Representatives.* US Congresswoman Judy Chu, June 19, 2012. Web. Accessed May 2, 2019.

Consider Your Audience

Adapt this passage for a different audience, such as your friends. Write a blog post conveying this same information for the new audience. How does your post differ from the original text and why?

FAST FACTS

- After gold was discovered in California in 1848, thousands of Chinese immigrants came to the United States.

- In the 1860s, work began on a transcontinental railroad. This project created thousands of new jobs. Many employers recruited Chinese laborers.

- The US economy collapsed in 1873. Competition for jobs increased. This created tension between white Americans and Chinese laborers.

- The Chinese Exclusion Act passed in 1882. It banned Chinese laborers from entering the country for ten years.

- During the early years of the Chinese Exclusion Act, some white Americans tried to remove Chinese people from towns and cities. These forced removals were called purges.

- In 1892 Congress passed the Geary Act. This act extended the Chinese Exclusion Act. The immigration ban was later expanded to include nearly all Chinese immigrants.

- The Chinese Exclusion Act was repealed in 1943. But a quota system still limited the number of Chinese immigrants allowed into the United States.

- In 1965 immigration quotas based on race were outlawed.

- In 2012 the House of Representatives passed a resolution. The resolution was an apology to Chinese Americans for decades of discrimination.

STOP AND
THINK

Surprise Me

Chapter Two discusses the events leading up to the passage of the Chinese Exclusion Act. After reading this book, what two or three facts about this history did you find most surprising? Write a few sentences about each fact. Why did you find each fact surprising?

Take a Stand

The Chinese Exclusion Act discriminated against Chinese immigrants. Think about current US immigration laws. How do you think people can address unfair immigration laws today?

Why Do I Care?

The Chinese Exclusion Act was repealed more than 70 years ago. But that doesn't mean you can't think about its relevance today. What are some attitudes about immigration that have been in the news recently? How are they similar to or different from what Chinese immigrants faced?

GLOSSARY

assimilate
to take on the values, traditions, and rituals of another culture

diplomat
someone who represents his or her country's government in another country

discrimination
the unjust treatment of a person or group based on race or other perceived differences

economy
a system in which goods and services are exchanged

immigrant
someone who moves from one country to another to live there permanently

lynch
to kill someone, usually by hanging

naturalize
to become a citizen of a country or nation

quota
a fixed number that is used to meet a requirement

racism
the belief that one race is superior to all others

transcontinental
something that runs across a continent

ONLINE
RESOURCES

To learn more about the Chinese Exclusion Act, visit our free resource websites below.

Visit **abdocorelibrary.com** or scan this QR code for free Common Core resources for teachers and students, including vetted activities, multimedia, and booklinks, for deeper subject comprehension.

Visit **abdobooklinks.com** or scan this QR code for free additional online weblinks for further learning. These links are routinely monitored and updated to provide the most current information available.

LEARN
MORE

Freedman, Russell. *Angel Island: Gateway to Gold Mountain.* New York: Clarion Books, 2013.

Zuchora-Walske, Christine. *The Transcontinental Railroad.* Minneapolis, MN: Abdo Publishing, 2017.

ABOUT THE
AUTHORS

Duchess Harris, JD, PhD

Dr. Harris is a professor of American Studies at Macalester College and curator of the Duchess Harris Collection of ABDO books. She is also the coauthor of the titles in the collection, which features popular selections such as *Hidden Human Computers: The Black Women of NASA* and series including News Literacy and Being Female in America.

Before working with ABDO, Dr. Harris authored several other books on the topics of race, culture, and American history. She served as an associate editor for *Litigation News*, the American Bar Association Section of Litigation's quarterly flagship publication, and was the first editor in chief of *Law Raza*, an interactive online journal covering race and the law, published at William Mitchell College of Law. She has earned a PhD in American Studies from the University of Minnesota and a JD from William Mitchell College of Law.

Kate Conley

Kate Conley has been writing nonfiction books for children for more than ten years. When she's not writing, Conley spends her time reading, sewing, and solving crossword puzzles. She lives in Minnesota with her husband and two children.

INDEX